SECRET
MILLIONAIRES
CLUB

SECRET MILLIONAIRES CLUB

Warren Buffett's 26 Secrets *to* Success *in the* Business of Life

ANDY and AMY HEYWARD

WILEY

Cover art: © 2013 A Squared Entertainment LLC
Cover design: Paul McCarthy

Published by John Wiley & Sons, Inc., Hoboken, New Jersey.

Published simultaneously in Canada.

Library of Congress Cataloging-in-Publication Data:

Heyward, Andy and Amy.
Secret millionaires club: Warren Buffett's 26 secrets to success in the business of life/ Andy and Amy Heyward.
pages cm
ISBN 978-1-118-49459-2 (cloth) ; ISBN 978-1-118-49461-5 (ePub);
ISBN 978-1-118-49447-9 (epdf)
1. Finance—Juvenile literature. 2. Finance, Personal—Juvenile literature. 3. Success in business—Juvenile literature. 4. Success—Juvenile literature. 5. Buffett, Warren—Juvenile literature. I. Title.
HG173.8.H49 2013
650.1—dc23

2013011246

Printed in the United States of America.
10 9 8 7 6 5 4 3

Contents

The Secret's Out ...!

Hi kids! My name is WARREN BUFFETT, a local investor around these parts.

I want to tell you about a very a special club where four 14-year-olds and a robot help other kids—and adults—answer questions and solve problems about money and business, as well as offering some really good advice that will serve you for a lifetime!

The club is *extra* special, not only because we help solve money problems for people all over the world, but also because it's a *secret*.

And that's why we call it *Secret Millionaires Club*!

Besides me, the club members are: RADLEY HEMMING, an African-American computer whiz; STARTY, a very cool robot that Radley built; ELENA RAMIREZ, a warmhearted teenager who dreams of working for the United Nations; JONES a freewheeling sports-guy who goes everywhere on his skateboard; and LISA, a Chinese exchange student who wants to be a fashion designer.

The kids might all have different dreams, but everyone in *Secret Millionaires Club* has one thing in common: an interest in learning about business and how it can teach valuable lessons that they can use as they embark on life's amazing journey.

Our meetings are held in a cool underground, high-tech conference room where we maintain our website, connect to the world, and stream the latest social networks on a giant video screen.

Speaking of video screen, we also have "D.E.B.", which stands for DEMAND EDUCATIONAL BASE—an online anthropomorphic encyclopedia that gives us access to all the knowledge that is out there by way of our laptops, digital tablets, smartphones, and other devices.

You might be wondering, how did *Secret Millionaires Club* form and what was the very first secret the kids learned?

Well, I'm glad you asked. . .

SECRET

#1

SECRET #1
Try to learn from your mistakes—better yet, learn from the mistakes of others!

Don't Be Afraid to Make Mistakes

Hi again. I'm glad you want to learn more about *Secret Millionaires Club*! In fact, the first lesson is all about learning!

When you own a business or manage a company, the last thing you want to do is make a mistake. You can lose customers *and* lose money by making too many mistakes. But sometimes slip-ups happen and a successful business manager learns from his or her mistakes.

It's the same thing in life. Learn from your mistakes—better yet; learn from the mistakes of others!

When school started last year, Radley, Starty, Lisa, Elena, and Jones had no idea that after learning this one simple secret, they would end up forming one of the most interesting and exciting clubs around: *Secret Millionaires Club*!

I met the four teenagers—and Radley's robot—on the first day of school because I was giving a pep talk to all the students. My message to all the kids was simple: "Even when you make mistakes, keep your eyes ahead—on the future. In fact, see your future. *Be* your future!"

Unfortunately, the school principal followed my speech with some bad news. Because of a lack of money, the eighth-grade field trip to New York City had to be cancelled.

Radley, Elena, Lisa, and Jones were upset, but at the exact same moment, they each came up with an idea for a fundraiser. They even made it a bit of a competition among themselves. Who could raise the most money and be the first to save the field trip?

But, try as they might, each of their moneymaking ideas failed. The four were so discouraged, they were about to give up, until I suggested that they work *together* and pool their ideas.

"Just toss out what didn't work," I said, "and focus on what *did* work!"

Radley, Starty, Jones, Elena, and Lisa combined their ideas and came up with a neighborhood popsicle delivery service that raised enough money to pay for the New York field trip! As an added bonus, they ended up meeting a friend of mine: the famous rapper Jay-Z!

When they returned home the kids were so excited that they had helped solve their school's money problems, they wanted to form a club—*Secret Millionaires Club*!

And together, we've been helping people around town and around the world ever since!

As I always like to say: "The more you learn, the more you'll earn," so remember:

SECRET #1

Try to learn from your mistakes—better yet, learn from the mistakes of others!

SECRET

#2

SECRET #2
Think twice before you either borrow money or loan money to someone—especially a friend.

Don't Borrow Money

Has anyone ever asked to borrow money from you—or, have you ever wanted to borrow money from another?

A business can get into a lot of trouble if its owners borrow too much money. This is especially true if money is borrowed to help a business grow, but then new sales drop and the company can't pay back its loan.

Borrowing too much money can get people into trouble too. If you borrow money to buy things that you want and don't earn enough money to pay it back, you can get into a big "money mess."

So remember: The best way to pay back a debt is to never have one.

The Daily Gazette - Homepage

THE GAZETTE

LOCAL YOUTHS HELP SAVE LOCAL NEWSPAPER

Jones and Lisa, of *Secret Millionaires Club*, learned this valuable lesson when the town's local newspaper, *THE GAZETTE*, was losing readers and almost went out of business.

Of course, *Secret Millionaires Club* kids wanted to help, and as they were brainstorming different solutions to the newspaper’s financial troubles, Jones had a problem of his own. He needed $25 to enter this year’s Mega-Monster Skateboard Contest.

Jones went to Radley, Lisa, and Elena for the money, confidently saying he would pay it back from the prize money—after all, he’d won the contest for the past four years.

Lisa agreed to loan Jones half the money she had saved for a new dress. But unfortunately, he lost the contest and couldn't repay Lisa's generous loan.

Jones and Lisa's friendship was suddenly strained—until I reminded them that their friendship was more important than squabbling over a debt.

Lisa decided she could create a unique outfit by spending the money she had left at a vintage clothing store. At the same time, Jones realized that he *had* to keep his promise to repay his debt, so he sold his favorite skateboard for $25.

Lisa was touched that Jones would sell his prized skateboard and told him to buy it back—*but,* Jones had to agree to a schedule for paying back Lisa's original $25 loan.

And to add to the happy ending, the *Secret Millionaires Club* kids convinced the troubled *Gazette* to cut printing costs and become successful again by adding an online version of their newspaper!

As I always like to say, "The more you learn, the more you'll earn," so remember:

SECRET #2

Think twice before you either borrow money or loan money to someone—especially a friend.

SECRET

#3

SECRET #3
Following your passion is
the key to success.

Love What You Do

When someone decides to follow their dreams, they have a better chance of being successful. Take for example, MRS. ROSE BLUMKIN, affectionately known as Mrs. B.

Mrs. B came from Russia with a dream to build a successful furniture business in America and she had a very simple approach: be honest, deal with integrity, and give the customers a bargain. Mrs. B followed her dream with excitement and passion—and absolutely *nothing* stopped her.

Starting with $500 Mrs. B built Nebraska Furniture Mart into the largest home furnishing store in North America and worked at the store until she was 103 years old!

Since we all need to work for a living, it's best to work at something you like. I love what I do and think everyone should pursue his or her dreams. One of the keys to success is to be excited about what you do and to always have a dream.

So remember: The person who can't be stopped, won't be.

As I always like to say, "The more you learn, the more you'll earn," so remember:

SECRET #3

Following your passion is the key to success.

SECRET

#4

SECRET #4
It is important to make the right trade-offs between work and play so we live a balanced lifestyle.

Make Time for Both Work and Play

Ever hear the expression: "Live a balanced life"?

In the business world, it's important for managers to be aware of the right trade-offs to be successful. You always want to invest in a business with managers who make good decisions.

Evaluating trade-offs and making the right decisions are also important in life—like choosing when to study, watch TV, be on the computer, or play video games. I recommend studying every day and trying to learn something you didn't know before.

So remember: It's important to make the right trade-offs between work and play so you can have a balanced life.

A few months ago, the *Secret Millionaires Club* kids learned this lesson when Lisa showed up for a meeting very distracted and run-down. It was clear that between homework, softball practice, taking pictures for a photography contest, and running in the Feetathon Race for Charity, Lisa was trying to do way too much.

At the same time, a local Italian cafe owner, ENZO, was spending every waking minute working in his restaurant. But no matter how hard and long he worked, Enzo couldn't get more customers into his restaurant. Like Lisa, poor Enzo was running himself ragged.

Radley, Elena, Jones, Starty—and yes, even Lisa—came up with lots of ideas for bringing in new customers, but nothing worked until both Lisa and Enzo realized that they needed more balance in their lives.

Keeping up with her schoolwork and running in the Feetathon Race for Charity were the most important things on Lisa's "To Do" list so she decided to drop off the softball team and planned to enter the photography contest *next* year.

At the same time, Enzo realized he missed visiting with friends and neighbors so he entered the Feetathon Race for Charity as well.

During the race, the chef was able to see old friends, make *new* friends, and tell everyone about his restaurant. And wouldn't you know it, after the race, his cafe was packed with customers.

From that day forward, both Lisa and Enzo dedicated themselves to only doing those things that were most important to them and to keep a balance between work and play!

As I always like to say, "The more you learn, the more you'll earn," so remember:

SECRET #4

It is important to make the right trade-offs between work and play so we live a balanced lifestyle.

SECRET

#5

SECRET #5
The experience of others is the best classroom you will ever find!

Listen to What Others Can Teach You

Who is your role model in life?

Most managers that are successful in business learned from someone called a mentor. A mentor—or "role model"—is like a teacher who shares their experience and guides others to become better at something. Choosing the right mentors in life—like your parents, grandparents, or a teacher—is important for success.

When learning from others outside of your family, you want to choose mentors who behave the way *you* want to behave throughout your life.

So remember: A handy trick to life is knowing who to be the batboy for—it's an important decision to make if you want to eventually be a homerun hitter.

Elena learned this lesson not by playing baseball, but from a simple pick-up game of basketball.

Elena is a very good basketball player, and during practice one day, she caught the eye of a sports scout named MR. STRINGER.

Until she met Mr. Stringer, Elena had planned to spend the summer taking a class for college, but he offered her a chance to go to a special teen basketball training camp called Peach Basket.

Well, Elena had stars in her eyes as she imagined herself becoming rich and famous as a professional basketball player.

But when Elena's idol, basketball superstar SHAQUILLE O'NEAL, dropped by to visit *Secret Millionaires Club,* he saw that she needed some helpful advice.

Shaq and Elena played a little half-court "one-on-one," and when Elena accidentally bumped into Shaq, he slipped and fell to the floor with a resounding crash. Poor Shaq rolled on the court, complaining about his ankle.

Elena was horrified that she had injured her hero, but then Shaq smiled and jumped to his feet.

"See how quickly an athlete can go from 'superstar' to 'out of work'?" Shaq chuckled. "As a sports pro, if you get seriously injured, your career could be over. But education—*education* lasts forever. Nothing can take that away from you."

Elena saw the wisdom in Shaq's advice, so she changed her mind, cancelled her plans to attend Peach Basket, and took not one, but *two* courses for college that summer.

As I always like to say, "The more you learn, the more you'll earn," so remember:

SECRET #5

The experience of others is the best classroom you will ever find!

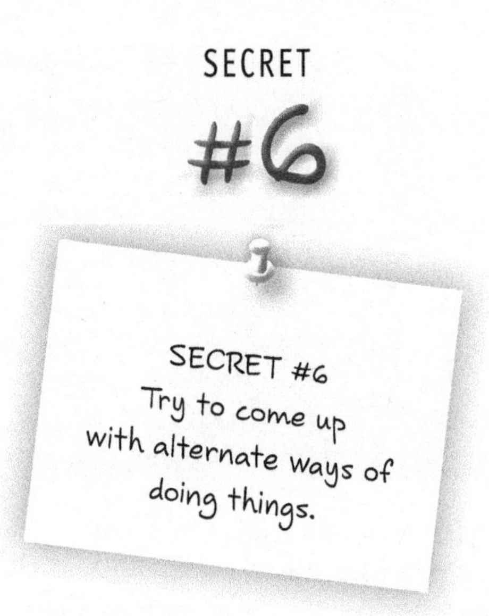

Always Think of New Ideas

It's easy to get in a rut and do the same thing over and over again.

In business, managers are always faced with roadblocks on how to grow their business or what to do when competition increases. The most successful businesses are constantly thinking of new ways to do things.

Thinking of alternative ideas and ways to do things is important in everyday life, too! Sometimes, when we try something for the first time, it doesn't work out the way we expect. Whenever that happens, be flexible and think of *other* ways to make something work.

So remember: It's best to think of new ways of doing things!

This secret really struck home when the *Secret Millionaires Club* kids formed a "virtual" band called THE LLAMAS. It was virtual because their drummer, a girl named MILLIE, lived in London.

A friend of mine, actor and singer NICK CANNON, helped Jones, Elena, Lisa, Radley, and Starty fly to England so they could shoot a music video with Millie.

Unfortunately, Millie wasn't in the mood to spend time with the band because her parents, owners of an old-fashioned record store, were arguing about how to save their business. Their store used to be very popular but now, with digital music downloads, most customers had stopped buying records and CDs.

The *Secret Millionaires Club* kids tried all sorts of ways to bring customers back into the store but nothing worked.

Right when all seemed lost, I suggested that they might be stuck using a bunch of old ideas to solve their problem and that they should try coming up with new and different ideas.

That one little suggestion was all they needed because the kids came up with a very imaginative idea: What if Millie's parents turned their old record shop into a modern dance club geared just for teenagers under 18 years old?

Millie and her parents *loved* the idea and it became an instant success.

And guess who performed on opening night? That's right; it was The Llamas themselves, with their very grateful drummer, Millie.

As I always like to say, “The more you learn, the more you'll earn,” so remember:

SECRET #6

Try to come up with alternate ways of doing things.

SECRET

#7

SECRET #7
When you fail to plan, you plan to fail.

Always Have a Plan

Now be honest with yourself, are you good at making plans?

Managers who carefully make plans for their business and then follow through with their plans tend to be successful. In other words, if a business doesn't properly plan how to make and spend money, it could end up failing.

Planning well is also important in everyday life. You need to plan for things if you want to be successful—like doing your homework every night so you can get good grades.

So remember: The will to prepare is just as important as the will to win—so if you fail to plan, you plan to fail.

This seventh secret was really important to learn when the *Secret Millionaires Club* kids traveled to Beijing, China, to visit Lisa's cousin, BOHAI.

From the very start of their trip Lisa, Radley, Elena, Jones, and even Starty failed to plan properly.

They didn't bring umbrellas and Beijing was in the middle of the rainy season; they packed the wrong electrical cords so they couldn't charge their phones and computers; and, as if that wasn't bad enough, Starty short-circuited in the rain and Radley had forgotten to bring along a spare set of robot parts.

To make matters worse, Lisa's inexperienced cousin Bohai was left in charge of his parents' grocery store and he mistakenly ordered dozens of crates of a special Chinese fruit called *zonzi*.

Lisa's cousin was so ashamed for spending all of his parents' money that he ran away from home and became trapped by rising floodwaters in the underground city of *Dixia Cheng*!

The *Secret Millionaires Club* kids, learning from their earlier mistakes, made detailed plans for finding and rescuing Bohai.

Once Lisa's cousin was returned safely home, our heroes suggested that his parents could make their money back by selling all the extra crates of *zonzi* to other grocery stores in the neighborhood.

So, not only did the *Secret Millionaires Club* kids learn to always plan in the future, Bohai also learned how to plan whenever he ordered more food for his parents' grocery store.

As I always like to say, “The more you learn, the more you’ll earn,” so remember:

SECRET #7

When you fail to plan, you plan to fail.

SECRET

#8

SECRET #8
Failure is not falling down;
it is staying down.

If You Fail, Try Again

Ready for another secret? It's all about being positive about failure.

A successful business is always trying new things—like trying to sell new products. But not every new product is successful and managers of a good business learn from failure.

"Trying new things" and knowing that you will make mistakes in life is important to understand—because *today's* failure can lead to *tomorrow's* success!

Think about it: What wonderful things could you do in life if you knew you could not be stopped by failure? Failing is not falling down; it is staying down.

And that's exactly what Elena learned when she raised a potbelly pig named TRUFFLES for the Fun Farm Yard Contest!

At first, Elena was confident and very organized. She created a simple budget on her smartphone to keep track of "pig food," "pig grooming," and "pig training." Unfortunately, Truffles became very, well, "piggish." Elena couldn't find a food her pig liked, or the right bath shampoo, or even the proper pig toy, so she panicked about losing the contest.

She dashed over to Pet's Pete Shop where PETE was having troubles of his own. He couldn't keep track of the pet supplies he ordered, so both Elena and Pete Junior thought of themselves as failures until I told them my favorite story about THOMAS EDISON.

When he was busy inventing the light bulb, Edison failed more than 10,000 times. But the great inventor never saw it as 10,000 failures, saying, “I just found 10,000 ways that *won’t* work.” In other words, Thomas Edison never let failure stop him.

With that helpful advice about never giving up, Pete Junior became determined to try again and soon discovered a simple way to keep track of ordering pet supplies.

At the same time, Elena discovered the right food for Truffles, as well as the proper shampoo and best pig toy ever. And Elena’s efforts were rewarded when she won a blue ribbon in the contest.

Back at *Secret Millionaires Club* headquarters, even Jones learned a lesson from Elena’s pig adventure, saying, “If I fail at least once a day, maybe I could be even *more* successful than Mr. Buffett!”

As I always like to say, “The more you learn, the more you'll earn,” so remember:

SECRET #8

Failure is not falling down; it is staying down.

SECRET

#9

SECRET #9
It takes years to build a reputation but only minutes to ruin it.

Protect Your Reputation

The next secret is all about what other people think about you.

One of the best things a business can do for success is gain a good reputation. Managers of businesses spend a lot of time winning over customers, employees, owners, and the community. They realize that a good business reputation is something that takes years to build—but they also know it can also be ruined in a minute!

Building a good reputation is important in life as well. The best thing you can do for yourself is to build a reputation for being kind, generous, and thoughtful to others. Make sure that you act as if everything you say, the things you do, and how you treat others could be posted on the Internet for the whole world to see.

So remember: A good reputation is the greatest thing to build over your lifetime—and make sure to never do anything to harm it in any way.

The secret about one's reputation made a big impression on the *Secret Millionaires Club* kids when they traveled to Scotland to help the owners of an old hotel, MCALLISTER CASTLE. The owners were losing customers because rumors had spread that a ghost was haunting the castle!

The ghost stories got started because of strange sounds and sightings at the castle. Fortunately, Radley, Starty, Lisa, Jones, and Elena weren't afraid to investigate, so they spent a night in the hotel.

After a few funny scares, our heroes realized there was a simple, logical explanation for every scary sight and sound at the castle. But when they showed our proof to the neighbors and unhappy hotel customers, they weren't convinced.

So to solve the hotel's financial problem, and attract a different set of customers, *Secret Millionaires Club* came up with the idea to advertise the castle as a creepy old place. In other words, they decided to play up the hotel's *reputation.*

Well, their idea worked, and new customers came from all over the world to spend time in a scary old castle—proving the power of one's reputation!

As I always like to say, "The more you learn, the more you'll earn," so remember:

SECRET #9

It takes years to build a reputation but only minutes to ruin it.

SECRET

#10

SECRET #10
Take care of your customer and your customer will take care of you.

The Customer Comes First

Do you listen carefully when others are talking?

A successful business is really good at communicating with its customers. And the best way for business managers to communicate with their customers is to ask a lot of questions and always listen to the answers. This way, a business can take care of its customers and the customers will take care of the business. Good communication is the key that allows a business to develop and grow.

As in business, you want to develop good communication habits in life by always questioning and listening. Keep asking "Why?" and "Why not?"—then listen carefully to the answers.

So remember: Good communication is important. Never be afraid to ask questions and listen to the answers—and also know that there is no such thing as a dumb question.

This particular secret came in handy when the *Secret Millionaires Club* kids traveled to Borneo—an island in Southeast Asia—to help an orangutan sanctuary and tourist attraction that was going out of business.

Our heroes met with ATAN, a teenager who ran the rescue park with his grandfather. Atan explained that his grandfather was good at taking care of the apes but didn't know how to attract more tourists.

Radley, Starty, Elena, Lisa, and Jones went straight to work repainting the sanctuary. Besides fixing the place up, and resupplying the gift shop with an assortment of flashy, modern souvenirs, our heroes enlisted help from world famous model GISELE BUNDCHEN to publicize the animal rescue park.

But even with all the changes to the sanctuary and Gisele's advertisements, more tourists failed to show up.

Luckily for everyone, during a walk through the local village, Gisele and our heroes noticed wonderful, handmade arts and crafts displayed by the locals. This gave the *Secret Millionaires Club* kids an idea: They would restock the sanctuary's gift shop with crafts from the village! Perhaps *that's* what the tourists preferred.

Sure enough, visitors began to flock to the sanctuary because they could not only support the orangutans, but also support the local artists!

The orangutan rescue park was saved and our heroes learned a valuable lesson in finding out what customers wanted. In the future, they would always ask questions, then listen to the answers!

As I always like to say, "The more you learn, the more you'll earn," so remember:

SECRET #10

Take care of your customer and your customer will take care of you.

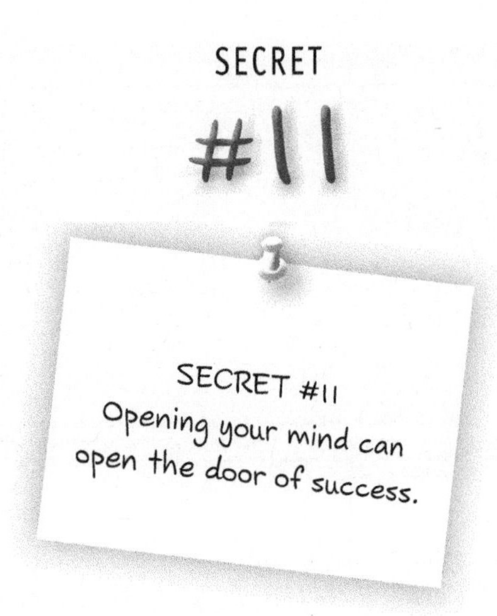

Open Minds Let In Better Ideas!

Is your mind open or closed?

In a successful business, managers show respect for others' opinions by encouraging different ideas. Put another way, these managers are *open-minded.*

By being open-minded, a business can create a positive environment for its workers by inviting everyone to suggest new ideas to improve the company and make it more successful.

In life, being positive and open-minded is also very important. It's always a better choice to be optimistic about the future and project a positive attitude.

So remember: Successful people look for new ideas. They don't automatically say "no"; they ask, "What are the terms and conditions of 'yes'?"

Radley learned about keeping an open mind when BILL GATES, a very successful businessman, visited *Secret Millionaires Club* headquarters.

Mr. Gates asked if Radley, Starty, Lisa, Elena, and Jones would travel to a small African village that didn't have electricity. He explained that if they could find a way to bring electricity to the village, the villagers would then be able to read books at night and access the Internet, as well as keep food and medicines cold.

Secret Millionaires Club was up for the challenge and, two days later, arrived at the village! It was nestled in a valley with a fast-flowing stream running beside it.

When Radley saw the stream, he had an idea for producing electricity: They could build a simple generator that was run by the flowing stream!

Just as Radley shared his idea, a village teenager named ADISU stepped up and offered to help him. Young Adisu had the same interests as Radley; he was energetic, inquisitive, and inventive. But since the two teens were so much alike, they immediately started arguing.

Radley was stubborn and insisted that they only use *his* design for the electric generator—even though Adisu said he had a better design in mind.

As Radley and Adisu continued to bicker, Starty, Jones, Elena, and Lisa stepped forward, accusing them both of not keeping an open mind. "If you keep up with your arguing," they said, "the village will *never* get electricity!"

Radley and Adisu saw the wisdom of their words and agreed to tackle the design together. They built a working hydroelectric generator that brought electricity to the entire village.

As I always like to say, "The more you learn, the more you'll earn," so remember:

SECRET #11

Opening your mind can open the door of success.

SECRET

#12

SECRET #12
Successful businesses successfully promote and advertise themselves.

Always Promote Yourself

Think about how you advertise yourself.

Every business needs to promote itself to sell its products and to distinguish itself from the competition. So it's very important for a business to *advertise* itself.

Did you ever think about this: You advertise yourself —meaning you project an image of yourself—every day by what you wear and how you treat others. It's important to advertise yourself in a positive way so people see you from the inside out. Always be honest and sincere, and never lie under any circumstance.

So remember: Treat other people the way you would like to be treated—that's the best advertisement of all!

The value of good advertising came to light when Radley, Starty, Lisa, Jones, and Elena were magically transported back in time to the kingdom of CAMELOT, where they met KING ARTHUR!

King Arthur needed help from *Secret Millionaires Club* because the good citizens of Camelot were having trouble making money.

As our heroes searched for answers to the problem, they came across a hardworking wheel maker named LEOFRICK SPOKES. Mr. Spokes was very good at making wagon wheels, but he didn't have any customers because no one knew about his business.

The *Secret Millionaires Club* kids came up with the perfect solution: Mr. Spokes should advertise his business by having town criers proclaim the quality of his wheels and by hanging banners with his company name on buildings and the sides of wagons!

Their suggestion worked, and before long, Mr. Spokes had dozens of new customers.

Promoting your business and yourself was just one of three important secrets that the club members discovered alongside the good citizens of Camelot, as you will soon see.

As I always like to say, "The more you learn, the more you'll earn," so remember:

SECRET #12

Successful businesses successfully promote and advertise themselves.

SECRET

#13

SECRET #13
Location is a vital part of most businesses.

Location Is Very Important

Have you ever thought about the importance of a good location?

Any business that sells to the public needs a good location so it can be found easily and is near the customers who want to buy its products.

And just as a store needs a good location to attract customers, *you* can benefit from being in a good location too!

In a classroom, it is best to sit in a place where you can hear the teacher and clearly see the lessons on the board. The better you are located, and able to pay attention, the better you will do in school.

Location, location, location—it can help you pay better attention and learn the most you can.

And as it turned out, the importance of location was another secret that *Secret Millionaires Club* learned when they were helping the citizens of CAMELOT with their money problems.

While escaping from an obnoxious dragon, our heroes got lost in the woods surrounding King Arthur's castle. Fortunately, they came across a skilled mapmaker named MARROK THE MAPMAKER.

Young Marrok had a variety of excellent maps to choose from and our heroes knew it would be easy to find their way out of the forest.

When they purchased a map, Marrok dropped to his knees and smiled, "You are my very first customers. Thank you, thank you, THANK YOU!"

Our heroes asked if Marrok was having trouble with his business. He complained that after spending months making maps he hadn't sold a *single* one before today.

Looking around at the surrounding woods, the *Secret Millionaires Club* kids instantly recognized Marrok's problem: He had set up his map stand in the middle of nowhere.

After they recommended that he move his stand into town, Marrok the Mapmaker became an instant success and—as with Mr. Spokes before him—became another successful businessman of Camelot!

As I always like to say, “The more you learn, the more you'll earn,” so remember:

SECRET #13

Location is a vital part of most businesses.

SECRET

#14

SECRET #14
If it seems too good
to be true, it
probably is.

Don't Be Fooled

Do you know when you've been fooled?

Managers of any business often receive offers on how to run their business, improve their sales, and make more money. Sometimes these promises are "too good to be true" and prove to be wrong—ending up hurting a business instead of helping it.

In life, as in business, you want to make sure that you carefully think things through when offered something. If someone guarantees that you will make easy money or they make promises that are unbelievable, then a warning bell should ring in your head. In other words, don't believe everything you hear.

So remember: Always be careful when considering a promise and always use good, common sense to make up your mind. If you think something seems too good to be true, you're probably right.

KING ARTHUR himself learned this secret when *Secret Millionaires Club* went back into time to visit him.

Arthur's kingdom, CAMELOT, had run out of money and the king was down to one small bag of gold. King Arthur planned to invest this last bag of gold and grow it into more money to help his kingdom.

Unfortunately, the king *almost* gave his bag of gold to a THIEF disguised as a prince.

The fake prince swore that he knew a wizard who could turn the king's one bag of gold into a hundred CHESTS OF GOLD! The fake prince only needed to "borrow" the king's gold for a day.

Fortunately, as the thief walked off with the bag of gold Radley, Starty, Lisa, Jones, and Elena said that his promise sounded "too good to be true."

Our heroes chased after the fake prince, recovered the bag of gold, and returned it to King Arthur so that he could invest it for the future.

As I always like to say, "The more you learn, the more you'll earn," so remember:

SECRET #14

If it seems too good to be true, it probably is.

SECRET

#15

SECRET #15
With businesses, like with people, you should get to know them before you judge them.

Don't Judge Others

Guess who? Right, Warren Buffett! Have you ever been misjudged by someone?

Managers of any successful business will go out of their way to get to know their customers before they introduce a new product or service. They never presume to know what their customers will like or dislike. In other words, they do not *misjudge* their customers.

It's also important not to misjudge people in your life. Make sure that you take the time get to know someone *before* you form an opinion about him or her. Prejudging someone because of how they look, what they wear, or by what others say about them is not a good idea.

So remember: Be careful not to misjudge others—most of the time it leads to a *lack* of good judgment!

This was an important secret that the *Secret Millionaires Club* kids learned when they traveled to Belgium to help a struggling young candymaker named JULIAN.

Julian, a skinny, sloppy young man, made the tastiest chocolate candies in Belgium, but he didn't know the best way to sell his candy to local candy lovers.

When Radley, Lisa, Elena, and Jones suggested that Julian partner with an older, established candy salesman, MR. VAN DEN BROCK, Julian immediately ran into trouble.

Mr. Van Den Brock mistakenly thought that Julian was so young and so sloppy-looking that he couldn't *possibly* be a professional candymaker. It was then that our heroes realized that Julian should present himself in a more professional manner.

Once Julian dressed into a suit and tie and cut his scraggly hair, Mr. Van Den Brock invited him into his shop to discuss the fine art of chocolate making.

When Mr. Van Den Brock sampled Julian's candy, he knew he had been wrong and apologized for misjudging Julian. The two candymakers became partners on the spot!

A lot of time was wasted because Mr. Van Den Brock had misjudged Julian—but the younger candy maker had also learned a lesson: When you want to be taken seriously in the professional world, you need to look professional.

As I always like to say, "The more you learn, the more you'll earn," so remember:

SECRET #15

Just like with people, you should get to know businesses before you judge them.

SECRET

#16

SECRET #16
Chains of habit are too light to be felt until they are too heavy to be broken.

Be Willing to Change Your Ideas

Ever thought you might have a few bad habits?

Business owners and managers always strive to be responsible and dependable. They try to think of how their actions today will affect their business in the days ahead and beyond.

For example, if a business borrows a lot of money for the short term but is not being able to pay it back, the results can be disastrous.

In life, another example would be if someone kept behaving in the same way—over and over—so that he or she never changed. This kind of behavior can cause problems if they don't see the advantage of "breaking the chain of habit" and acting differently.

So remember: Do your best to be responsible and dependable—and if you think you are developing any bad habits, try to break them.

Radley, from *Secret Millionaires Club,* learned this secret when he had to break one of *his* "chains of habit."

It all started when Radley planned to enter this year's Science Fair contest. He was excited about telling Jones, Lisa, Elena, and Starty his idea for building a new robot.

Unfortunately, his buddies thought it sounded very, very boring. And when Lisa suggested that Radley could win the

Science Fair trophy with a different kind of robot—one with lots of style and flair—he grew very quiet.

Even when Jones and Lisa agreed with Lisa's idea and suggested that Radley become partners with her, he resisted, arguing that he had *always* made his own Science Fair projects and he wasn't going to change now! Radley had gotten into the habit of always doing things by himself.

Radley stubbornly kept to himself and drew designs for his boring robot. When he displayed them for everyone, they almost fell asleep—all except Lisa. She brightened and suggested that Radley could give his robot an interesting outfit. "Better yet," she chirped, "what if you built a robot that changed digital outfits instantly?"

Now it was Radley's turn to get excited as he realized Lisa had a terrific idea. "It would be a 'Fashion Bot'!" He smiled as he shook Lisa's hand. "Let's make it together—partner!"

So Radley and Lisa built the Fashion Bot together and they won the Science Fair trophy!

As I always like to say, "The more you learn, the more you'll earn," so remember:

SECRET #16

Chains of habit are too light to be felt until they are too heavy to be broken.

SECRET

#17

SECRET #17
Price is on the price tag; value is in the eye of the beholder.

Your Image Is Important

It's never too early to improve your image.

A service business, such as a restaurant, works hard to create an image so that when customers think of the business, they know they'll have a "good experience." This experience could be good food, good service, or a fun setting—or all three!

When a good image is reinforced through advertising, the business can become successful, since customers will go out of their way to eat there for the good feelings. In other words, the restaurant makes them feel happy!

This happens in real life, too. You should work on your image so that you have a good reputation and people only think "good things" about you!

So remember: The best thing you can do to improve your image is to be likeable—someone who is honest, kind, and thoughtful of others—an all-around good person.

Secret Millionaires Club stumbled upon this secret when they traveled to Stockholm, Sweden, to help a tiny restaurant called DAHLQUIST that was going out of business.

The family-run eatery specialized in dishes featuring a small, local fish: the herring.

After having lunch with the owner, MR. DAHLQUIST, Radley, Starty, Lisa, Elena, and Jones recognized that the setting was terrific, the service was good, and the herring dishes were delicious. *Secret Millionaires Club* was stumped. Why didn't Mr. Dahlquist have more customers in his restaurant?

Then they saw an advertisement for THE HAPPY HERRING, a huge restaurant chain that specialized in fast-food herring dishes.

Our heroes checked out The Happy Herring and the place was packed! It was noisy, bright, and colorful, and the customers were happily eating their herring sandwiches.

What was the big difference between the two restaurants? Then Radley had a brainstorm. The Happy Herring advertised itself on TV, on banners—everywhere! "That's it!" Radley exclaimed. "Dahlquist needs to do the same thing."

So *Secret Millionaires Club* helped Dahlquist restaurant advertise on the Internet, with banners at all the local sports events, and through the newspaper. The key to the success of the advertising was that it pointed out how unique Dahlquist was compared to The Happy Herring.

The restaurant soon had customers lining up outside to get in. *Secret Millionaires Club* had done it again!

As I always like to say, "The more you learn, the more you'll earn," so remember:

SECRET #17

Price is on the price tag; value is in the eye of the beholder.

SECRET

#18

SECRET #18
If your service is outstanding, you'll always stand out.

Be Thoughtful of Others

Want to know how to make even more friends?

One of the best ways for a business to stand out is for it to be respectful of its customers, to care for them as if they were friends. Customers almost always prefer to do business with companies that treat them with respect.

Being nice and making friends is also important for success in life. You should always strive to be nice, care for others, and be friendly; if you do this, you're sure to stand out.

So remember: The first *three* rules for making friends are: Be pleasant, be respectful, and care for others. The *fourth* rule is to pay attention to the first three rules!

This particular secret came to light when *Secret Millionaires Club* learned that their local soccer team, THE SWANS, was losing money so it was being sold and would probably move out of town!

Radley, Starty, Lisa, Jones, and Elena were shocked. Not only were The Swans the only professional soccer team around, they served the world's best pizza at Swan Stadium! Our heroes dashed to the stadium to see if they could help the team raise money so they wouldn't be sold.

When our heroes arrived, they immediately knew that things had changed at Swan Stadium. Trash littered the ground and the concession stand had stopped selling hot dogs—and the pizza tasted terrible!

To make matters worse, the owner, MR. FELLUM, stopped playing music during the games and the Swan mascot—a fan favorite—was no longer performing.

Our heroes met with Mr. Fellum and suggested that the problem might be that the stadium and team had stopped being a service to its fans and therefore showed that it didn't care about them. *That's* why no one came to the games anymore.

Mr. Fellum saw the wisdom of what they were saying and things changed immediately. The soccer players threw a big thank you party for their fans, Mr. Fellum had the stadium cleaned and repainted, and the pizza was once again the best in the world.

After the soccer team showed its appreciation for its fans, the fans returned to Swan Stadium in droves. With the seats filled to capacity, there was no reason to sell the team, so The Swans stayed right where they were!

As I always like to say, "The more you learn, the more you'll earn," so remember:

SECRET #18

If your service is outstanding, *you'll* always stand out.

SECRET

#19

SECRET #19
A good business is disciplined to do the little things right every day.

Pay Attention to Details

Do you pay attention to the little things in your life?

For a business to be successful, it needs to be disciplined to do all of the "little things" right. In other words, follow through on all the details of its business—every day. This gives customers confidence that the product or service they are buying will be what they expect.

Discipline and practice are also important for individuals to succeed in life. If you do all the little things right every day, then the big things will follow. For example, studying every day will make learning at school a lot easier and you will become smarter. Practicing a sport or activity will only make you better at it. Also, exercising every day helps you to stay healthy.

So remember: If you want to be good at something, you need to be disciplined and keep practicing. If you take the easy way out by cutting corners and doing things too quickly, you'll never be as good as you could be!

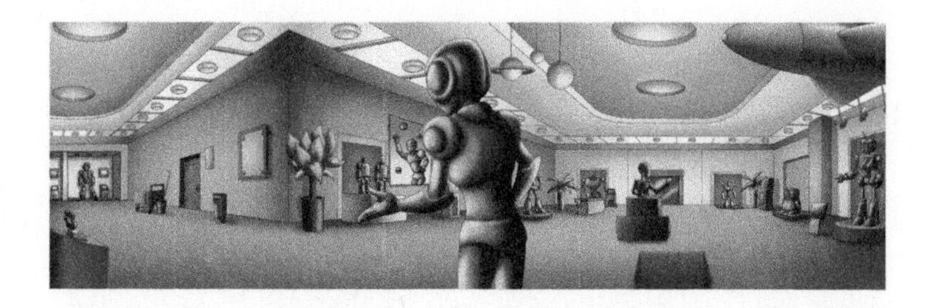

Two weeks ago, Radley certainly learned this secret when small objects started disappearing around *Secret Millionaires Club* headquarters. Radley volunteered to solve the mystery—even though Jones wanted to jump in and help him.

The mystery continued when our teenage heroes visited ROBOSITY MUSEUM, a local museum specializing in robots.

During their tour of the museum, things began to disappear from the exhibits. Without doing much investigating, Radley claimed that the museum janitor, MR. OTTO VON OTTO, was behind all the disappearances.

But when Jones persuaded Radley to bear down and carefully look at all the clues—all the details of the disappearances—he discovered that his robot, Starty, was malfunctioning and had been hiding everything he could get his little robotic hands on!

Radley quickly fixed Starty's programming and all of the missing items were returned—including the items from *Secret Millionaires Club* headquarters.

Radley learned that he should have focused on the job at hand and studied all of the details of the case, and he could have solved the mystery much faster!

As I always like to say, “The more you learn, the more you’ll earn,” so remember:

SECRET #19

A good business is disciplined to do the little things right every day.

SECRET

#20

SECRET #20
It's not just the outside that counts. It's the whole package.

How to Present Yourself

How you present yourself is very important.

Every business needs to "package" itself in order to become successful. How a business appears on the outside tells a customer a lot about how it acts on the inside.

That's also a life lesson. Packaging yourself properly is also important. It's like having a scorecard showing on the outside that reflects your *inner* scorecard.

For example, you should show respect if you want to be respected. Admire honesty as part of being honest. And be lovable to be loved.

Remember: The outside reflects the inside and the inside reflects the outside—both are a reflection of the whole package!

This important secret came to light when *Secret Millionaires Club* went skiing during their winter break.

Once Radley, Starty, Lisa, Jones, and Elena arrived on the mountaintop they were shocked to see that their favorite ski lodge had changed. The new owner, MR. LUKAS, had transformed the lodge from a simple American hotel into a flashy Swiss ski lodge! Everything was now Swiss: the design of the hotel's exterior, the design of the rooms, the uniforms worn by the staff, even the menu, which only offered Swiss foods.

It turned out that our heroes weren't the only ones disappointed with all the changes. The lodge was almost deserted when they arrived, and guests were checking out left and right.

And with lots of guests leaving, all of the other businesses in town were failing as well.

Something had to be done, so our heroes explained to Mr. Lukas that his business had plummeted because all of the local skiers preferred the look, the feel, and the services of the *original* ski lodge. In other words, they didn't like how he had changed the outside and the inside—the packaging—of their favorite ski lodge.

Taking advice from *Secret Millionaires Club*, Mr. Lukas converted the lodge back the way it was, the skiers returned, and it became a popular winter resort once again!

As I always like to say, "The more you learn, the more you'll earn," so remember:

SECRET #20

It's not just the outside that counts. It's the whole package.

SECRET

#21

SECRET #21
Make sure you stay in school. Failing to complete your education can lead to not achieving your dreams in the future.

Your Decisions Affect Your Future

Ever heard of the domino effect?

When managers of a business make decisions, they have to think of the consequences. It's possible that a decision that is made today can have a "domino effect" on the future. In other words, just as one domino can knock down a row of one hundred dominos, one decision can have an impact on events the next day, next week, and on into the future.

For example, if a manager decides to charge too much money for a product, then—BANG!—it might lead to lower sales and—BOOM!—lower sales may lead to—KABANG!—making *less* money.

This secret also applies to your life. A decision you make today might affect events in your future. The best example that comes to mind is that you should stay in school, because failing to complete your education *today* can lead to *not* achieving your dreams in the future.

Remember: One decision can affect your future—just like one little domino can knock down a row of one hundred dominos!

The importance of this secret was made clear to *Secret Millionaires Club* when singer KELLY ROWLAND dropped by their headquarters. She needed their help to organize auditions for her new School of Performing Arts.

Radley, Starty, Jones, Lisa, and Elena happily volunteered to help and, while they were at the auditions, one 14-year-old performer really stood out.

Her name was LUCINDA and she sang like an angel. In fact, when Lucinda finished her audition, Kelly and the *Secret Millionaires Club* kids jumped to their feet knowing that she would definitely make it into Kelly's School of Performing Arts.

But when the amazing young singer was asked to fill out an application for the school, she panicked and ran from the auditorium!

Our heroes caught up with Lucinda outside, where she admitted that she had dropped out of school because she wasn't very good at reading or writing. Lucinda had given up on school a year ago and there was no going back.

But then Elena told her the story about a single domino and added, "A positive decision you make *today* just might pay off in the *future!*"

Lucinda broke into a smile and decided to give school, and her future, another chance.

As I always like to say, "The more you learn, the more you'll earn," so remember:

SECRET #21

Make sure you stay in school. Failing to complete your education can lead to not achieving your dreams in the future.

SECRET

#22

SECRET #22
Save money for things you need instead of spending it all on things you want!

Save for the Future

Want to know the secret of how your money can make money by itself?

Managers need to save money for advertisement, for supplies, or to buy equipment so their business can grow in the future. But if a business doesn't save money and spends all that it earns, it can eventually go out of business.

Saving money is also a very important habit for you to form as early as you can. As you earn money, you should get into the practice of putting some aside so you can buy the things you need in the future.

In other words, as Ben Franklin once said, "A penny saved is a penny earned!"

The *Secret Millionaires Club* kids learned this secret on a very exciting day: the day they opened a small savings account for their club.

Just as Radley, Starty, Lisa, Elena, and Jones electronically placed a dollar each into the club's new savings account they were visited by SOJ, a female inventor from 300 years in the future!

Radley, the club's computer nerd, wanted to hear about how her time machine was designed, but Soj had a much more pressing issue to discuss.

In her own time, Soj had gotten a bank loan so that she could build her time machine in the first place. But she was now in trouble because she had spent all the money instead of saving part of it or planning how to pay the loan back. Now her loan was due, and if she failed to repay the money, the bank would take her time machine away!

Our heroes hopped aboard the bizarre-looking machine and flashed to the future, where they met with the bank manager, MR. UTRA. Mr. Utra calmly explained that Soj had just five minutes to repay her loan.

Soj began to panic, but the *Secret Millionaires Club* kids calmly started coming up with ideas for a solution to her problem.

Lisa was the first to realize that the $5 they had placed in the club's savings account in present day had been growing for 300 years and was now enough money to pay for Soj's loan!

Our heroes allowed Soj to use their club's savings to pay back her loan so that she could keep her time machine.

So both Soj and the *Secret Millionaires Club* kids learned a valuable lesson about putting away money today to save for the future!

As I always like to say, "The more you learn, the more you'll earn," so remember:

SECRET #22

Save money for things you need instead of spending it all on things you want!

SECRET

#23

SECRET #23
Prices are determined by supply and demand.

Be Someone in Demand

You're doing a great job following all these secrets! Here's a basic one about business—and life!

Businesses sell—or "supply"—products at prices determined by how many buyers want it—that's called "demand." If a lot of buyers want to buy the product, the seller can charge more money for it, and that's called "the Law of Supply and Demand."

In life, we are all subject to the simple law that there are two things that everyone can supply without limitation: knowledge and love. Do your best to share both of these with others—especially your family.

Remember: Share your knowledge freely and be lovable. In other words, *supply* all the positive things in life to others and you will definitely be in *demand.*

Secret Millionaires Club learned about the secret of supply and demand on the day four ordinary-looking black and white puppies wandered into their headquarters.

When the frisky puppies became too much to handle, Radley, Starty, Lisa, Jones, and Elena decided to give them to PETE, the owner of PETE'S PET STORE.

It turned out that the puppies had actually escaped from the pet shop and Pete was delighted to get them back. But try as he might, Pete couldn't sell a single black and white pup.

The *Secret Millionaires Club* kids tried everything they could think of to help Pete sell the dogs to a good home, but there just weren't any buyers.

After doing some research, our heroes discovered that there just wasn't enough demand by buyers for ordinary black and white dogs—and the lack of buyers meant no sales for Pete.

But then Jones found a place that was glad to take the puppies—it was a DOG ASSISTANCE TRAINING CENTER, which trained dogs to help disabled people, people who were blind, those in wheelchairs, and the elderly.

And for such a good cause, Pete decided to supply the puppies for free.

So in the end, Pete's pups were not only in great demand, but they ended up with loving owners.

As I always like to say, "The more you learn, the more you'll earn," so remember:

SECRET #23

Prices are determined by supply and demand.

SECRET

#24

SECRET #24
Don't get involved in
a business you don't
understand.

Confidence Comes with Understanding

There's a lot of power in understanding others—and yourself.

Good managers truly understand their business, understand what their competitors are doing, and understand what their customers want. This kind of understanding helps successful businesses adapt to change.

And understanding is also important for success in life! For example, understanding what is needed to complete a task or being able to understand another person's point of view. And while you're at it, be prepared to change your mind if *their* point of view makes good sense.

Remember: Learn to understand something before you do it. In other words, think things through before you act.

Radley, the techno-geek member of *Secret Millionaires Club*, learned this secret when he, Starty, Lisa, Jones, and Elena visited ROCKET INCORPORATED. It was a brand-new business that planned to launch tourists into space!

Radley was the most excited among the club members because he dreamed of becoming an astronaut. The owner of Rocket Incorporated, ZACH Z. ZACHARY, invited Radley to try out its astronaut-training program but, unfortunately, Radley failed each and every step of the course.

This happened just as all three of Rocket Incorporated's space tourists cancelled their reservations.

None of them had a full understanding of space travel: One tourist was afraid of heights, another hated the thundering engine noises, and the third tourist couldn't fit inside the rocket.

Zach took responsibility for not properly informing his customers about the details of their flight, and with all the cancellations, announced that Rocket Incorporated might be closing before it even got off the ground.

But the *Secret Millionaires Club* kids, with an understanding of what Rocket Incorporated could accomplish, put their heads together. Radley presented their idea to Zach: "Instead of tourists, what if your rocket carried supplies from Earth to the International Space Station?"

Zach liked the suggestion, so he switched the goals of his business and rocketed to success.

And what of Radley? He understood that even though he might not be astronaut material, he *was* talented enough to plan the flight to the space station and made all the calculations necessary for docking the rocket ship. Radley had a future in the space program after all!

As I always like to say, "The more you learn, the more you'll earn," so remember:

SECRET #24

Don't get involved in a business you don't understand.

SECRET

#25

SECRET #25
Be smarter at the end of the day than you were at the beginning.

A Lifetime of Learning

Did you know that learning could last you a lifetime?

For a business to be successful in the long run, managers need to constantly learn—learn more about their customers, their competitors, and changes that are always happening in the marketplace.

In life, it's the same thing. I've often said that the best investment you can make is in yourself—and to do that, challenge yourself to learn something new *every* day.

Remember: Learn to be better at what you like to do and that will make you happy with yourself. And if you are happy with *yourself*, others will be happy with you!

Elena and Lisa learned this secret when the *Secret Millionaires Club* kids took a trip to eastern Africa.

Their plane made a forced landing in the middle of a banana plantation due to an approaching thunderstorm. Once they were safe on the ground, they met an African teenager named AKEELA, and her mother, AFAAFA.

While chatting over tea, Radley, Starty, Lisa, Elena, and Jones learned that Afaafa's banana plantation had a business problem. Her husband had died recently, and since men in this part of the world rarely worked for a female boss, the male laborers, who owned the only truck in the area, had left the plantation and taken their truck with them.

So the problem was, how would Afaafa and Akeela transport the bananas to market before they spoiled?

Lisa suggested that Afaafa get a bank loan to buy a truck. Afaafa and her daughter laughed. "As with the male workers, the banks in this country won't give a loan to a woman."

Radley, Starty, Lisa, Elena, and Jones wondered if Afaafa had looked around for *other* ways to get a loan and she replied, "Why bother? It wouldn't be of any use."

Knowing that one never stops learning, our heroes did some research and discovered a new financial trend in Africa called "microloans." These were very small amounts of money, sometimes as little as $50, that were loaned to women to get them started or keep them going in a business.

Together, Afaafa, Akeela, and the *Secret Millionaires Club* kids found a microloan lender and Afaafa was able to buy a truck to carry the bananas to the market.

And the best surprise was when Elena showed Radley that she knew how to repair the truck engine, proving that you can learn something new every day!

As I always like to say, "The more you learn, the more you'll earn," so remember:

SECRET #25

Be smarter at the end of the day than you were at the beginning.

SECRET

#26

SECRET #26
Great partnerships will make any job easier.

Partners Make it Easier

Well, here we are—the last secret. Isn't it easier to do things with a partner than doing them alone?

For a business to be successful, it needs a lot of people to work together smoothly. So building good relationships and having first-rate partners is important.

In life, it's also a good idea to build partnerships to be successful—especially with your friends and family.

A great partner makes any job easier.

Working with partners came up last summer when *Secret Millionaires Club* spent a week at CAMP BIG FOOT. They were disappointed to see the camp looking old and run-down, but before they could offer to help, they were hustled off to their separate cabins by two bickering counselors—CHUCK and his sister, GIGI.

That night the camp owner, BRUCE, mentioned that the camp was in desperate need of more money, and then told a campfire story about the legendary creature, BIG FOOT! "If there really *was* a Big Foot," Jones joked, "your camp would bring in *lots* of campers and your money problems would be solved!"

Amazingly, the next morning Chuck found footprints that looked like they belonged to Big Foot himself! Chuck and Gigi were again competitive about who could find proof of Big Foot the fastest—ending with everyone exploring the woods that night.

When the group was frightened by growling and rustling in the trees, they jumped into a canoe and were swept up onto an island with no way to signal for help!

As Radley, Starty, Lisa, Elena, Jones, Chuck, and Gigi searched for a way to get off the island, they discovered a huge carved statue. Radley recognized it as a carving by early Native Americans.

After finding the giant carving, Chuck and Gigi confessed that *they* had faked the Big Foot footprints so that curious campers would come and fill up the camp. "Good thing your plan *didn't* work," Elena sighed. "A fake Big Foot would have ruined the camp's reputation and made matters worse!"

Our heroes then recommended that Chuck and Gigi, being the oldest, work together to climb a tree and signal the distant shore. A rescue party saw their flashlight signals and pulled them off the island.

Once safe, Chuck and Gigi congratulated themselves for working together and *Secret Millionaires Club* had a brainstorm to save the camp. Instead of a fake story about Big Foot, the camp could have special tours to see the American Indian artwork!

The promotion idea worked and the camp quickly filled up, as Chuck and Gigi agreed to always work together as partners.

As I always like to say, "The more you learn, the more you'll earn," so remember:

SECRET #26

Great partnerships will make any job easier.

About A Squared Entertainment

A Squared Entertainment is an entertainment company dedicated to producing "content with a purpose" for kids. In today's digital age, entertainment for kids is no longer a passive activity. Kids interact with media and A2 creates purposeful content that is as entertaining as it is enriching and engaging. In partnership with one of the greatest, and wisest, "value investors" of all time, A2 created *Secret Millionaires Club* to help kids better understand the world around them. The goal was not to teach kids to read a balance sheet, but rather explain how business functions, with situations they can relate to. And, impart some valuable life lessons along the way that will serve them a lifetime.

We are eternally grateful to Mr. Buffett, who was instrumental in creating the original "curriculum" that served as the foundation for the TV series and this book, a collection of valuable and easy-to-understand life lessons to help guide kids to develop healthy habits from a young age. Lessons like:

"The best investment is an investment you make in yourself."

"The more you learn, the more you'll earn."

"It takes a lifetime to build your reputation, and five minutes to ruin it."

"Find something you like to do, and you'll never work a day in your life."

"Risk comes from not knowing what you're doing."

It's never too early to develop good habits that will last a lifetime, and we hope that *Secret Millionaires Club* will help kids discover that they already have the power to live the life that they dream of.